JUST AN ORDINARY LAWYER

A Monodrama with Songs
For A Male African Actor-Singer
With Live Piano Accompaniment

by Tayọ Aluko

Published by Playdead Press 2017

© Tayọ Aluko 2017

Tayọ Aluko has asserted his rights under the Copyright, Design and Patents Act, 1988, to be identified as the author of this work.

A CIP catalogue record for this book is available from the British Library.

ISBN 978-1-910067-44-4

Caution
All rights whatsoever in this play are strictly reserved and application for performance should be sought through the author before rehearsals begin. No performance may be given unless a license has been obtained.

This book is sold subject to the condition that it shall not by way of trade or otherwise, be lent, resold, hired out, or otherwise circulated without the publisher's prior consent in any form of binding or cover other than that in which it is published and without a similar condition including this condition being imposed on the subsequent purchaser.

Playdead Press
www.playdeadpress.com

Just An Ordinary Lawyer was commenced by Tayọ Aluko as Leverhulme Writer-on-Attachment at Liverpool Everyman and Playhouse Theatres in 2014, and received seed commission from Theatre Royal Bury St. Edmunds and Black Theatre Live in 2016.

It was first performed on 4th August 2016, at Spotlites on George Street, Edinburgh, during the Edinburgh Festival Fringe 2016.

CAST:

Written and performed by	Tayọ Aluko
Director	Amanda Huxtable
Dramaturg	Esther Wilson
Designer	Emma Williams

with Gus Carmichael on piano

Tayo Aluko | Writer + Performer

Tayo was born in Nigeria, and now lives in Liverpool. He worked previously as an architect and property developer, with a special but as yet frustrated interest in eco-friendly construction. He has fronted orchestras as baritone soloist in concert halls, and has also performed lead roles in operas and musicals. His first play, *Call Mr. Robeson* has won numerous awards in the UK and Canada, as well as highly favourable reviews in the press – most notably in *the Guardian* and on BBC Radio 4. He has toured the play around the UK, the USA, Canada, Jamaica and Nigeria. He also delivers a lecture/concert called *Paul Robeson – The Giant, In A Nutshell*, and another one titled *From Black Africa To The White House*: a talk about Black Political Resistance, illustrated with spirituals. He researched, wrote and narrated to camera a piece on West African History before the Trans-Atlantic Slave Trade, which forms part of the permanent exhibit at Liverpool's International Slavery Museum. His 15-minute play, *Half Moon*, which also deals with ancient Africa, has been performed several times in the UK. He has been published in *The Guardian*, *The Morning Star*, *NERVE Magazine*, *Modern Ghana* and *Searchlight* Magazine. *Just An Ordinary Lawyer* is his second full-length play, and was premiered at the 2016 Edinburgh Fringe.

Angus Carmichael | Piano

Gus Carmichael B.Mus./P.G.C.E, studied piano with Audrey Innes from St Mary's Music School and David Parkhouse from London. His musical interests and styles are very broad. He was accompanist for the folk singer Mary

Sandeman, worked as session keyboard player with the late Billy Mackenzie and has accompanied Rowan Atkinson. He performs concerts for Music in Hospitals, works with performing arts students at Edinburgh College, accompanies singers/instrumentalists, plays in a jazz quartet and teaches piano.

Amanda Huxtable | Director

Amanda trained at Manchester Metropolitan University, Recreational Arts in the Community course, followed by studying for a BA Degree in Communications and Cultural Studies at The University of Leeds. She continues to strengthen her practice by studying Social Sciences and The Arts, Past and Present at the Open University. Amanda served as Artistic Director of Yorkshire Women Theatre Company in Leeds 2004-2009. She enjoys being part of a writer and director team with Marcia Layne and together they run Hidden Gems Productions a theatre company committed to telling rarely told Black British Stories, Black British and Bold, and is building her portfolio of freelance directing work across the UK..

Theatre Directing credits for Hidden Gems Productions tours 2010-2016 include; *Bag Lady*, *Somebody's Son*, *Lost & Found*, *The Yellow Doctress*, all by Marcia Layne. Freelance Director credits include; *The Promise* by Chris Cooper (Belgrade Theatre Tour), *The Dressmaker's Gift* by Anita Franklin (Liverpool's Write Now International Festival), *Totally Over You* by Mark Ravenhill (Lawrence Batley Theatre), *Continent Chop Chop* by Virtual Migrants, *HD100*

(Chol Theatre), *Just An Ordinary Lawyer* (Tayo Aluko in association Theatre Royal, Bury St Edmunds and Liverpool Everyman & Playhouse). Associate Director on *Wakefield Mysteries* adapted by Nick Lane, directed by Andrew Loretto (Theatre Royal Wakefield) *Lady of Situations* by Shirley Harris and Seniveratne, Vanitas Arts (Off The Shelf Festival and Sheffield Arts Exchange). Amanda is the proud recipient of an Arts Council Change Makers award that will support her time as Artistic Associate at Hull Truck Theatre until 2018.

Emma Williams | Designer
Emma trained as a theatre designer at Wimbledon School of Art and has worked extensively for touring companies, most recently with Hidden Gems on *The Yellow Doctress*, *HD100* for Chol at the Lawrence Batley theatre, both directed by Amanda Huxtable; *Iyalode of Eti*, Utopia Theatre; *Molly's Marvellous Moustache*, *Fidget* and *You Forgot the Mince*, Imagine Theatre. Designs for the West Yorkshire Playhouse between 2003-2015 include: *Immune*; *Nine Lives*; *Refugee Boy*; *You The Player*, co-production with Look Left Look Right; *Scuffer*; *Crap Dad*; *Two Tracks and Text Me*; *Runaway Diamonds*; *Broken Angel*; *Sunbeam Terrace*; *Huddersfield*; *The Dutiful Daughter* – co-production with Szechuan People's Theatre, Chengdu, China; *Coming Around Again*; *The Elves and The Shoemakers*; *Pinocchio*; *The Magic Paintbrush* and the original version of *The Yellow Doctress*. Other designs include *One Among Millions*, co-pro between RJC Youth Dance and Leeds University, 2016; *Brief Encounters @*

Bradford Interchange, a site-specific piece for Freedom Studios; *Somebody's Son*, Hidden Gems; *Strawberries in January*, Traverse, Edinburgh; *The Shoe*, Polka Theatre; *The Swing Left*, Unlimited Theatre; *Small Objects of Desire*, Soho Poly Theatre. Opera credits include: *Siroe*, Royal College of Music; *Partenope*; *Admeto*; *Alceste* all for Cambridge Handel Opera at New Hall Cambridge; *La Cenerentola*; *The Tales of Hoffman* and *Genevieve de Brabant*, French Institute, London.

Esther Wilson | Dramaturg

Esther writes for stage, TV & radio. Her first R4 play *Hiding Leonard Cohen* won a Mental Health in Media award. *The Heroic Pursuits of Darleen Fyles* is an on-going series for Woman's Hour on R4. Her stage play *Soulskin* toured nationally with Red Ladder. She was lead writer on the award-winning *Unprotected*. *Ten Tiny Toes* was shortlisted for a TMA award. In Collaboration with Paula Simms, Esther worked on *The Quiet Little Englishman*, set in a disused cinema, for Liverpool's Capital of Culture. The piece was hugely ambitious and critically acclaimed. The sequel to the R3 version of Tony Teardrop was commissioned by R4. Esther's TV work includes: Jimmy McGovern's *The Street* (RTS award for best newcomer), *Accused*, *Moving On*, *Call the Midwife* and *The White Princess*.

For a long time now, I have been writing a paragraph in my programme notes at almost every performance *Call Mr. Robeson*, relating Paul Robeson to today's world. This tradition has so far continued with Just An Ordinary Lawyer, starting with its premiere at the Edinburgh Fringe. I reprint the four done so far at the time of publication of this script.

JUST AN ORDINARY LAWYER. A play, with songs. Written and performed by Tayọ Aluko, with Gus Carmichael, piano Spotlites @ Edinburgh Fringe. Thursday 4 August 2016 (World Première)

"The world seemed to be disintegrating around us," is one of the first lines delivered by Tunji Ṣowande, looking back at 1968 from the 1980s. It is sobering that those words and the stories he tells resonate so strongly with today's situation. As one watches the horrors going on round the world, one is struck by how the reporting and analysis leave out (often deliberately) the history behind the conflicts. It is my intention to make a modest contribution to the fight against this ignorance, both by highlighting why nationals of former imperialist powers need to shed their continuing arrogance, and by presenting stories of those who heroically fought against occupation, injustice, intolerance and racism, particularly in the context of Africa and the Diaspora. However, as I hope the play demonstrates, we make little progress if we don't recognise the humanity in all others, recognising that their struggles are our struggles too, whoever they or we are. One may be horrified by the prospect of who may end up leading the most militarily powerful country in the world in the coming years, but as the play reminds us, the world has seen pretty awful situations before, and people have triumphed, not least through art and love – truly the most precious, effective, natural and enduring weapons and gifts we possess, which we really need more of.

JUST AN ORDINARY LAWYER. A play, with songs. Written and performed by Tayọ Aluko, with David Dear, Piano. Liverpool Playhouse Studio, October 4 – 8, 2016

I must confess to being very irritated by parts of the coverage of the Rio Olympics in August. It was bad enough it being made to look as if we were turning up and switching on to watch Great Britain take on the rest of the world, but the constant insinuation that Team GB were practically the only ones immune from the foul play and corruption that plagues other countries, and that honesty, probity and fair play are somehow a uniquely British trait. As we have recently been reminded by goings on at the top of British Football, this is not necessarily the case. Furthermore, if one goes beyond the field of sports, into other aspects of life and into history, one will be reminded that much of what "made Britain Great" is the stuff of which the British can hardly be proud. Greed, deception, cruelty and brutality played no small part, along with the manufacture and use of (and the profiteering in) lethal weapons. Latterly, amnesia has crept into the national psyche too, such that the revelation of darker aspects of the national history comes as a shock to many. In contrast with the arrogance of a great number of Europeans, the psychology of far too many of us from Africa and the Diaspora has been so adversely affected by the distorted history that we have imbibed, either from formal education or otherwise, that we even believe things to be the way they are today because of failings or inadequacies in us as a race. Rather than being able to identify the real enemy therefore, we resort to fighting among ourselves, or accepting the status quo, forgetting that many of the freedoms we enjoy now are the product of brave struggles by ordinary and extraordinary people who went before us. We therefore watch with horror and bafflement as the violence in the world seems to plunge to new depths, without remembering that arms-trading companies here and abroad, with the full support (and indeed, connivance) of governments here, continue to reap obscene profits, and escalate and perpetuate the carnage and destruction for the sole benefit a small number of people who can only be described as evil. In the eyes of many elites, the scariest, most dangerous weapons are far too easily accessible. These include inquiring minds, knowledge of history, the arts, and love. It is my hope that in using art to share inspiring stories of ordinary people doing extraordinary things, we are reminded that regardless of where we were born, and where we operate – be it on the field of sport or any other arena, we have the ability, individually or collectively, to unleash powerful forces for good.

JUST AN ORDINARY LAWYER. A play, with songs. Written and performed by Tayọ Aluko, with Philip Blandford, piano. Burdall's Yard, Bath, Tuesday 25 October 2016

This morning, there was news about the current International Development Secretary once more wishing to cut the overseas aid budget, arguing that it needs to be more efficiently spent, and used to promote business enterprise. The meagre amounts being spoken of are but a teardrop in relation to the billions available at the drop of a hat to prosecute wars in those very parts of the world that strangely never seem able, after many decades, to get their act together. Naturally, if people on the other side of the world can't develop in the way that Great Britain has developed, the question needs to be asked why all this money is being spent on the undeserving poor? The fact that Britain developed, and continues to prosper relatively at the expense of peoples with whom they have had contact over the last several centuries tends to be conveniently forgotten in such conversations. The nature of the foreign interventions that has led to this state of affairs is really quite shocking, and, it must be said, shameful. Still, as an African proverb reminds us, the best way to treat a boil is to lance it. In other words, expose the dirt, clean it out, and release the pressure that would otherwise cause a messy, unpleasant explosion. Confronting the sordid truth is uncomfortable but necessary, and it is this that this play seeks to do in a small way, in the hope that it might generate interest in finding out more, and creating a better understanding of why inequalities of wealth exist between nations, and indeed within nations, such as this one. The stories of many heroic people who have struggled and sacrificed so that people like me enjoy the kind of life and opportunities that exist today need to be retold, to inspire the next generation of fighters for freedom and justice. They exist in all walks of life – the sporting field that we are particularly interested in today being but one. The world of politics is another, although when one sees a minister whose name suggests that her background is from one of the parts of the world that Britain colonised, it is becomes clear that no section of society is free of the urgent need of learning more about colonial history, or indeed owning up to it, and the fact that the exploitative project requires collaborators from within the victimised populations. It requires the rest of us to arm ourselves with knowledge, and determination to continue the struggles of those who went before, to honour our debt to them.

JUST AN ORDINARY LAWYER. A play, with songs. Written and performed by Tayọ Aluko, with David Carlston Williams, piano Bolton Socialist Club, Friday 26 October 2016

Dangerous times are in store for our brothers and sisters across the Big Pond. There is not only the unenviable choice they have to make about who will be their next leader, but also the fact that foreigners are once more entering their territory, bringing disease, violence and destruction in their wake. The invaders I refer to are not Mexicans or other nationals seeking safety and opportunity in the socalled Land of the Free, but oil companies who have recently been seen using para-military force against Native Americans and their supporters trying to block the laying of the oil pipeline across their sacred territories in North Dakota. It is impressive how bravely and non-violently these people have conducted themselves in the face of corporate and state violence, and how well they have argued their case (seemingly to no avail) that great environmental, spiritual and physical damage will be the inevitable result of this pipeline. However, despite centuries' worth of history that teaches us that people who live simply and are better connected to the earth are infinitely wiser than the rest of us as they argue that people and water are much more precious than money and oil, the state carries on with its rapacious behaviour. People of African descent should have little difficulty in identifying with the Native Americans, having seen their Mother Continent violated in this way for centuries, and this play is an attempt to help reconstruct the stories firstly of exploitation that has led to all sorts of ills that have befallen Africa and her peoples as they have been scattered around the globe, and secondly to pay tribute to some of the heroic figures that resisted the forces of tyranny. Their stories and those of similar people around the world inspire us to join and support those who continue to resist all forms of exploitation in whatever way we can. It may indeed still be worth praying for the future of a planet where in the most militarily powerful nation, the best democracy money can buy somehow manages to deny its wisest, most peace-loving and caring citizens (not to talk of the most vulnerable) the peace and power they deserve.

Author's Note

A friend in Liverpool had been telling me for years about his uncle who sang – a hobby I shared. He had apparently also told the story of once singing with Paul Robeson, whose story I have been telling in *Call Mr. Robeson* to some acclaim for nine years. Several years after this "Uncle Tunji" died, I inherited much of his sheet music too. That friend, Fẹmi Ṣowande sent me a short, interesting Wikipedia write-up done by a Nigerian historian, Ed Keazor. I subsequently met Ed, saying that I might one day do a play about Tunji Ṣowande. This was back in 2011.

Two years later, Liverpool Everyman and Playhouse Theatres invited me to submit a 15-minute musical for their EveryWord Festival. I had never written a musical before, but I accepted the challenge, and came up with something called *Kwamina's Song* – based on a story told by a white Liverudlian sailor who, when they were shipwrecked, had his life saved by an African who passed him a floating barrel and himself drowned. That young Liverpudlian was Edward Rushton, who became a poet, founder of the Royal School for the Blind (he contacted ophthalmia from the captives) and fervent abolitionist. *Kwamina's Song* seemed to impress the Everyman and Playhouse, and they invited me to be one of their Leverhulme Writers on Attachment.

I submitted a few play ideas to work on, one of which would have Tunji Sowande as the protagonist. Secretly, it was not my favourite idea, because from what I had gathered, Mr. Sowande was not a political man, and thanks to Paul Robeson's influence, I consider myself a socialist.

Conversations with people who had worked under him (Kim Hollis QC, John Perry QC, George Adonis, Charles Digby and Kim Bale) and other members of his family – his daughter Mrs. Ayo Eneli (now deceased) and Granddaughter Ezim Eneli all confirmed this, but each gave me interesting stories about him. These always included his love of cricket, and his pride in being a member of the MCC (Marylebone Cricket Club). Wondering how many Black members there were in his time, I enquired with two people there – Neil Robinson and Sarah Gillett, and got not that information on Black membership but other valuable bits.

When my research led to a friend, book collector and dealer Tony Aitman lending me a book on Basil D'Oliveira, I had finally found the key that would unlock the door, and the play started pouring out. Amanda Huxtable came on board as director, with Esther Wilson as dramaturg and Emma Williams as designer. Mark Loudon came out of semi-retirement with a nice lighting design. Karen Simpson of Theatre Royal Bury St. Edmunds decided to put me forward for a Black Theatre Live seed commission, Liverpool Everyman and Playhouse gave us rehearsal space, and I premiered it at the Edinburgh Fringe in August 2016, with Angus Carmichael on piano.

Getting a 5-star review in the first run of an untried play is tremendously encouraging, and I am filled with optimism for its future. I thank all the people and organisations mentioned (and those who contributed financially and in other ways) for their part in helping bring the story to life. I hope that it is entertains, educates and inspires those who experience it, on stage, or on these pages.

Tayo Aluko.
Liverpool, December 2016

The setting is what looks like a private study in a home, or a barrister's or judge's chambers in the mid 1980s. At the piano, stage right, THE PIANIST is playing a medley of West African-inspired piano pieces and/or Spirituals as audience awaits the start of the play. Some books, files and papers and a cricket ball on a desk at stage left. A vintage swivel executive chair on wheels at centre stage. Downstage right, a coat stand with a hat, a coat, maybe a barrister's gown, wig etc., and a cricket bat.
Blackout.

In the dark, we hear a ticking clock, and a cappella singing on stage:

> I got shoes, You got shoes, All God's chillun' got shoes

Lights go up to reveal Mr. TUNJI ṢOWANDE, retired barrister in his early 70s, on stage. SOWANDE is dressed very smartly, in a three-piece suit, black slip-on brogue shoes. He wears a white shirt and a self-knotted bow tie. A handkerchief in his jacket pocket. He paces slowly as he sings. He takes out a pocket watch, looks at it for several seconds, as if waiting for the second hand to reach twelve.

> When I get to heab'n gonna put on my shoes

He closes and puts the watch away.

He picks up the bat and starts to practice some strokes, then speaks. His manner of speech is very proper – refined English, with only a hint of a Nigerian accent.

ṢOWANDE:

One of the most thrilling cricket matches I ever attended was at the Oval, London, in August 1968. It was the second day of the fifth and final Test in the England / Australia Ashes series. The ground was packed to capacity. People were following BBC coverage all over the country, and of course, in Australia. They were also listening particularly keenly, at all levels of society, in South Africa.

1968 was one hell of a year. The world seemed to be disintegrating around us. Martin Luther King and Bobby Kennedy were killed. Rioting all over the United States. France too, with general strikes. *(Replaces bat)* A war of attrition between Israel and the PLO. Anti-Vietnam War Protests everywhere. The Soviet Union invaded Czechoslovakia. And Nigeria was in the middle of a bloody civil war.

(Beat. Sits)

You may well ask why I, a Nigerian barrister, was at the Oval on that day of all days, with the world seemingly falling apart? Why I felt no guilt taking the day off to be there? Well, this was no ordinary cricket match. It was history in the making. A fine cricketer had just played an innings that would have repercussions beyond the boundaries of that ground, beyond the game itself, into international politics. An innings which had shown civilisation at its best – the aesthetic beauty of a wonderful game. The grace and artistry of a player at the height of his powers, rising to a great occasion. Basil D'Oliveira had just been dismissed after scoring 158 runs for England, and I was on my feet with the rest of the crowd, applauding him as he walked into the pavilion.

As I turned back round, still clapping, my eyes met those of another man I hadn't seen in almost twenty years, but despite the years, and the ten yards that separated us now, it was instant recognition. We stared at each other for about two seconds. Long enough for me to feel his disdain and contempt again. After all that time.

(Beat.)

Funnily enough, I also associate him with one of my fondest memories, because just a few months after I arrived in London in December 1945, I had attended an audition in the very same square in which I first met him: Red Lion Square, London WC2. I had heard that a small Christian organisation were auditioning singers, for nursing homes, in Conway Hall, one Saturday.

I arrived at 10.55, and was eventually shown into this large room. Two ladies were behind the desk in the middle, the piano and pianist at one end. They had been deep in conversation but looked up.

(As if staring, open-mouthed)

I broke the silence.

"Good morning. Tunji Sowande is the name. I would like to sing for you The Holy City, by Stephen Adams."

Song: THE HOLY CITY

> Jerusalem, Jerusalem
> Sing for the night is o'er

> Hosanna in the highest
> Hosanna for evermore
> Hosanna in the highest
> Hosanna for evermore

I am pleased to say I was hired, and have sung in Nursing Homes regularly ever since —in London, and the provinces. So very rewarding to be able to bring some pleasure to the old dears, but I find it strange that the British seem so ready to abandon family like this. It is one thing we don't do in Nigeria.

I have been singing that song for almost sixty years! First as a boy treble in the choir at CMS Grammar School (Church Missionary Society) in Lagos, about 1923. The masters were all British, and Mr. Vaughan sang the solo. I sang it when I transferred to King's College at sixteen, by which time I had become a baritone.

KC, as it was known, was where my other great love, cricket, really developed. We had played it at CMS, but King's were the undisputed masters, the champions – throughout West Africa, in fact.

(Beat.)

After King's, I studied pharmacy, got married, had two children, Ayọ and Tunde, and set up in business with a former classmate. Our business did quite well, but to tell you the truth, I wasn't a happy man. My marriage was, shall we say, difficult, and I yearned for classical music, and cricket. And then I pictured myself as an old man with an even older wife, having done nothing more than sell imported chemical drugs. So, even at age 33, I decided to train as a barrister – and I would do it in London. I would do more music. Enjoy cricket, visit the great grounds I had read and heard about: the Oval; Old Trafford; Edgbaston; Headingly, and Lord's, the home ground of the MCC, and the home of cricket. I would at last be able to watch international teams – South Africa, Australia, New Zealand, The West Indies.

The West Indies... *(Chuckles)* My mother said to me as I was leaving, *"Ma lọ f'Ajẹreke o!"* Please don't marry an *Ajẹreke*. *Ajẹreke* means "sugar cane eater." We saw them as children of slaves, you see – not appreciating the fact that sugar was the crop they were enslaved to grow. But I knew better. Why? Because they were great cricketers, and often held their own against the likes of England and Australia. So, in that respect at least, they were as good as anybody else.

(Beat)

You know, if not for some small accident of fate, it is possible that one of my direct ancestors could have wound up in Jamaica or Haiti, or Alabama or Mississippi? That is if they even survived the Middle Passage.

(Pause)

Isn't it interesting that those that did survive, despite the multiplicity of cultures and religions they took with them, most ended up becoming followers of Jesus Christ, and some of their descendants would return to the land of their forefathers as Christian missionaries! And they brought with them those beautiful songs which we know today as Negro Spirituals.

I recall one English lady in a Braintree home telling me of having been a missionary herself, and teaching the native children – her words – in Rhodesia some spirituals. She was in this particular home for about three years in the 1960s, and I made a point of singing this next one for her each time I visited. I would say, "And specially for Mrs. Pane, *DEEP RIVER.*"

> Oh, don't you want to go
> To dat gospel feast?
> Dat promised land
> Where all is peace?
>
> Oh, Deep River
> My home is over Jordan
> Deep River, Lord
> I want to cross over into camp ground.

It turns out that some twenty years earlier, Mrs. Pane and I had arrived in Liverpool on the very same ship: she to retire, I to start my new life. I had sold my share of the business to my partner, and persuaded my mother to take in my daughter, Ayọ. She couldn't have my son, Tunde, alas, because he was only three, and needed to stay with his mother.

(Beat)

Two weeks before I left, I had taken them to Bar Beach on Tunde's birthday. He had such fun:

"Mu ball, mu ball!" *(Action of throwing a large ball to his son)* *(Clapping)*, "Ọmọ dada!" I thought, "My boy will grow up, the ball will get smaller, he'll become a great cricketer, and I'll watch him play for Nigeria, at Lord's!"

(Beat)

So, to London. I loved it from the start, but ooooh, it was cold! The music scene was so vibrant. Thanks to my brother, Fẹla and other contacts, I sang here, there and everywhere, and enjoyed an active social life. Being unattached again was a, er, a help.

I passed the bar exams first time, started applying for legal positions, and started coming up against the colour bar. I got a steady stream of rejections but persevered, and about ten months after my exams, I got called for my first interview, at Castlemount Chambers, Red Lion Square. I was so excited! I couldn't afford a new suit, but I did buy a new bow tie.

I was kept waiting for twenty four minutes beyond the appointed time – 10am -before being shown to the office of Edgar Mappin Esq., one of the younger Heads of Chambers in London, at fifty.

(Simulated dialogue)

"Enter!"

(Pause)

From the photographs, it was clear he was also a keen cricketer. One showed the MCC committee at the House of Lords, and there he was among them. Another was the 1930 Oxford University team at Lord's before their match with the MCC. There was also a cricket bat, signed by the 1934 Australian Test team, including the great Donald Bradman – a name I knew from my schoolboy days in Nigeria. "This is wonderful," I thought, "I'm going to fit in just fine at Castlemount Chambers. We'll discuss cricket over sherry in the club on a Friday evening…"

"How do you say your name?"

"Ọlatunji Ṣowande, Sir… Oar lah toon gee Show wahn day"

"That's a rather difficult name to pronounce, isn't it? Why don't you use a good English name like the West Indians do?"

"But that's my name, sir. It's the name I was christened with. I –"

"How are my clients supposed to react when I tell them I'm sending a junior along with a brief, and that he is called Mr Tumba Tumba Shomba Gomba? They'll know I'm sending an African, will they not? What will that say about us, huh?"

And then he looked up at me for the first time, with… condescension.

"Now, look here. I know you Nigerians are coming here in increasing numbers for your education, but as far as I know, most of them get it and go straight back home. You say in your letter that – where is it? Yes – 'I hope to establish myself as one of the first African barristers in London, and pave the way for others who wish to contribute to the smooth running of the profession in the hallowed courts of England,' end quote. Well, I suggest you leave English courts to English gentlemen, get on the next boat, and go and establish yourself back home in Bongo Bongo land. Miss Glover will see you out."

(Beat)

I was transported back to King's College. Mr. Hyde-Johnson, the Principal and cricket coach was reminding the team how cricket is the quintessential gentleman's game. The game that showed British values at their best - immaculate whites; clapping the other team in and out, congratulating an opposing batsman when he reaches a landmark score; and most importantly, the honesty and decency expected of a batsman, who having faced a delivery, knows that the ball touched the bat ever so gently that only he and maybe the wicket keeper who has caught it behind him know it. There is an unspoken rule, a code of gentlemanly conduct, which is, "You get a nick, you walk." That means you admit it and declare yourself out by starting to walk back to the pavilion. "You get a nick, you walk."

I was now back in this London office, and this, gentleman, this, this gentleman... cricketer – had just spoken to me in the most unexpectedly uncivil way!

"Good day... Sir" was all I could say. I stumbled down the stairs and out into Red Lion Square, in a daze. Why did I let him get away with that? I should have told him, gently, calmly, and with all dignity, that I was not just another Blackie. That I was an Old Boy of King's College, Lagos, from a highly respected Yoruba family. My brother, Fẹla, was one of London's most celebrated organists and composers. I had been a successful pharmacist, a father of two, a singer, and like him, a cricketer. I deserved – no – demanded, more respect… That's what I should have said.

I found myself walking past a group of Africans outside the London School of Economics. One of them introduced himself as Ladi Williams. Apparently, they were part of the West African Students' Union (WASU). There was a meeting going on inside on the state of emergency in Kenya, where several leaders of the Mau Mau had been imprisoned. He suggested I went in, but as I was due to catch the 1.27 to Norwich for a nursing home concert that afternoon, I had to make my apologies. If that Edgar Mappin hadn't kept me waiting for twenty four minutes, I could have learned more about what perceived wisdom described as a terrorist organisation, heard why they refused to go through legitimate processes put in place by the British Government, insisting instead on killing innocent white people and terrorising their fellow countrymen. I didn't say any of this to Ladi of course. He sold me a copy of their paper, *News Service*, saying I should be sure to read the letter he had had published in that edition. We exchanged contact details, and I continued on my way.

Another two months passed, and luckily, I was introduced to a distinguished barrister, Jeffrey Howard, QC at church. He invited me to his Inner Temple chambers later that week. He couldn't have been more different from Mr. Mappin. You see, it turned out he had visited the Gold Coast often as a boy, and had in fact fallen in love with a girl there, but wasn't allowed to marry her.

So, I finally had the pupillage I had been trying a whole year to find! I spent my first six months shadowing Mr. Howard, the second six on my own, and finally, I became Ọlatunji Ṣowande Esquire, Barrister-at-Law, Inner Temple. I was assigned most of my cases through the Dock briefs in court. Many of my clients reacted with apparent unease when they first saw me, but they had no choice. Without exception, I prepared and argued my cases diligently and well, and a further six months later, was formally confirmed as a tenant at 3 King's Bench Walk!

One of my more memorable cases dates back to 1954. My client had been accused of involvement in a West End robbery, but he had a cast iron alibi, but one that couldn't be made public. On the night in question, he was actually in Nairobi, not London. He had gone on behalf of His Majesty's Government, under an assumed identity, with diplomatically cleared luggage containing cash. British Pounds. His mission? To – shall we say – recruit willing Kenyans to testify against one Jomo Kenyatta, implicating him in being a leader in the Mau Mau. On the basis of this fabricated evidence, Kenyatta and others in the liberation struggle were jailed, without the British Government's involvement coming to light. How to prove my client's innocence without jeopardising British National Security? In the end, I didn't have to, because I was able to establish inconsistencies in the prosecution's submissions (basically the police fabricating crucial evidence) and the case was thrown out.

This was disturbing! For one, legal and security protocols prevented me from mentioning any of this, though the facts are now in the public domain. Secondly, I realised for the first time that the British Police were not as squeaky clean as I had hitherto assumed. Thirdly, I was confronted with irrefutable evidence that the British Establishment were (in this case at least) in bed with the criminal class, and that the British Empire of which I was a loyal subject was trying desperately to hold on to its colonial possessions by any means – fair or foul – and that the foul would often override the fair!

(Beat)

I had kept Ladi's letter to *News Service* from three years earlier. *(He searches in the desk, stumbles across an envelope which clearly distresses him. He pauses briefly, puts it aside and finds what he was really looking for – a box of clippings, and selects one. Reads, in a strong Nigerian accent)*

"Sir, The trend of events in Kenya serve as a stark reminder (if any were needed) that British politicians' promises are palpably empty at best, and grotesquely cynical at worst. Do our so-called colonial masters think we have forgotten how their loyal subjects were persuaded by the hundreds of thousands to join the Great War against Fascism, with Churchill and Roosevelt's Atlantic Charter promising self-governance, only for them to be told on their return that it was never intended for African peoples? Was it not the same

British government that caused the deaths of twenty-eight brave ex-servicemen in Accra in 1947 for demonstrating in demand of pensions at the promised levels? No! No reminder is needed that any trust invested in the word of representatives of His Majesty's Government, be they Tory or Labour, is trust gravely and carelessly misplaced."

(Chuckles) Ladi was allegedly a medical student, but he seemed to spend most of his waking hours as an activist - at meetings, demonstrations and marches, and always writing to whoever would publish his letters. I suspect that he might even have been a, a Communist, like many of the WASU members. Each to his own, I say. Ladi also loved reading. Mainly on African history and politics. The man was a font of knowledge. In the end, he gave up medicine and became a book collector and dealer in Hackney. He never made money, but he was happy, because he was surrounded by books, and was "contributing to the education of the common man." His proudest, happiest moment was when none other than Dr. Martin Luther King, Jr. visited his bookshop, signed some books, and posed for photographs with Ladi Williams.

And by far his saddest was King's assassination. Actually, Ladi had predicted it – he said that talking about dreams of equality was fine, but denouncing poverty or the Vietnam War was crossing the line, and that "they would silence him." And silence him they did. April 4th, 1968.

Song: I DREAM A WORLD.

> A world I dream where black or white,
> Whatever race you be,

Will share the bounties of the earth
And every man is free,
Where wretchedness will hang its head
And joy, like a pearl,
Attends the needs of all mankind-
Of such I dream, my world, my world, my world!

I became Head of Chambers in June 1968. The news was carried in *The Barrister's Magazine*, and there was a little paragraph in the Times, headlined, "NIGERIAN BECOMES FIRST COLOURED HEAD OF CHAMBERS IN BRITISH HISTORY." WASU wanted to throw a party in my honour, but I wouldn't have any of it. I didn't want any fanfare. I was just an ordinary lawyer who wanted to do good.

One way in which I tried to do that was by giving young barristers their chance to get a foot on the ladder. Some who were finding it difficult to get tenancies because of the colour of their skin. John Perry, from Jamaica. Kim Solarya from Ceylon – now Kim Hollis. Being female didn't help her either. McKee Wright, from Ghana. George Adonis, from Cyprus (now, he looked suspiciously white to me). A good, talented bunch. They've all done well. They responded well to guidance. *(Beat)* Unlike Tunde… I'd offer him some fatherly advice, and he'd end up shouting at me. And what's worse, I'd often find myself shouting right back…

I had a policy of allocating celebrity briefs to my juniors. I personally didn't want a high profile. I decided it didn't pay to be too obviously talented and successful as a Black man.

Sometimes White people don't take too kindly to it – they get jealous. Lay traps. Sabotage you. And the bigger the threat you are seen to pose, the more inconvenient things can get, especially if you are militant. Like Paul Robeson, Muhammad Ali. In extreme cases, they can even kill you. From Toussaint L'Ouverture in Haiti to Patrice Lumumba in Congo, to Fred Hampton in the States.

Don't get me wrong. I am happy to do my bit in the court room when called upon, or lend support financially or by contributing a song now and then, but militancy doesn't always pay. One can be quiet about things, but still eloquent with one's actions. Now, Basil D'Oliveira personified this, this quiet eloquence.

Being Cape Coloured, he couldn't play first class cricket in his native South Africa, so with the help of John Arlott, the famous English commentator, he travelled to England to join Middleton, a league club in Lancashire, as a professional. This was 1960. And would you know it, by 1968 he had already played in three Tests for England!

Then, it suddenly dawned on everybody that he might very soon be eligible to play against South Africa – *in* South Africa! The country where sixty nine Black protesters had been killed in the Sharpeville Massacre just before he left. Where Mandela and many others were languishing in jail on Robben Island. Who only White international teams – Australia, New Zealand or England played, with Coloureds and Blacks only allowed to watch from the "coloured" sections. Suddenly, the prospect of D'Oliveira returning to play on grounds he had never been allowed to walk on began to emerge!

But strange things were happening to him in England. He had played well against Australia in the West Indies earlier that summer, had top-scored in the first Ashes Test at Old Trafford. But he was then left out of the second, third *and* fourth tests. Could it be that the selectors were worried about South Africa? Surely not. Then, as luck would have it, injury and illness among the squad meant that he was finally called up for the fifth Test, with England one nil-down, and therefore having to win to square the series. He came in at number 6, with 238 runs on the board, and finished that evening on 24 not out. Quite a cliff hanger!

(He picks up the bat and starts to demonstrate) The following morning, he proceeded to steadily pile up runs, knocking the ball to all areas of the field. Intelligent, strong, and elegant. His fifty came before tea. Each run a slap in the face of the apartheid regime. A slap in the face of their Prime Minister, John Vorster, who had declared that they would not welcome an England side that included D'Oliveira. His century came just after lunch. With each and every run, everybody knew that his place on the England team was becoming increasingly secure. The best team to tour South Africa *had* to include D'Oliveira, but – were the South Africans bluffing? Could they, would they actually cancel the tour? He reached 150 with a beautifully executed leg glance for two. His cricket was so confident, so natural, so gracefully easy.

He continued after tea with four singles and another four. Then he went for another big hit off Mallett, but he didn't quite middle it. The ball went up in the air for an easy catch by Invererity at mid-off. A majestic innings had finally ended with 158 glorious runs. 158 bullets into the body of Apartheid South Africa. The crowd immediately got to its feet and applauded him all the way off the pitch, the Australians too. Up the steps, people patting his back as he passed them. He must have been ecstatic, despite the restrained, controlled smile.

As he disappeared into the pavilion, I turned round still clapping, and that's when I spotted Edgar Mappin. Our paths had not crossed since the day he humiliated me in his office eighteen years earlier. He was now His Honour Judge Mappin, QC, I was now Head of Chambers at 3 King's Bench Walk, and here we both were at the Oval, after all that time. Sitting there in his MCC blazer, arms folded, he had that same look of contempt from the last time. He turned away, and I too sat down to watch Brown start his innings. He didn't last long, making just two runs before being dismissed, ending a respectable England innings. I looked across and saw that Mr. Mappin was no longer there.

The next day was the final day. England needed to get Australia all out. By lunch, they had already taken five wickets, for only 86, but then... an almighty downpour. The ground was flooded, and it looked like it would end in a draw after all, giving the series to Australia 1-0. The rain stopped at about four o'clock, and we waited for another hour, hoping the pitch would drain dry. Everybody except the Aussies, that is! The England captain, Colin Cowdrey, went out to inspect with the head grounds man, and realising the pitch wouldn't dry out after all, got on a megaphone and appealed to the crowd to come and help dry it manually, and they did! They swept water away with brushes, mopped up with blankets and towels, collected water in cool bags. The colour bar came down too. Most of the Blacks took off their shoes, rolled up their trousers and joined in!

And me? I thought about it. But I was now the Head of an Inner Temple Chambers. I am never seen in public without a jacket and bow tie. And one can't wear a tie without shoes and socks, can one? Besides, there were photographers, and TV cameras around. And a war raging in Nigeria. No, it wouldn't do for me to be seen like that. Not in front of all those people, those cameras, and certainly not with my country at war.

So I watched on as the spectators became chorus actors in this mini epic drama. The match eventually resumed, and England won it, squaring the series.

That same evening, the MCC committee met to choose the England side. They deliberated till the early hours of the following morning, and the selection was announced the following day. *(Beat)* D'Oliveira had been left out.

(Beat)

The outcry was immediate and deafening. The selectors didn't know what had hit them. Try as they might to argue that their decision was not influenced by South Africa, nobody believed them.

Even in Parliament, MPs denounced them for bowing to political pressure. Committee members and ordinary members resigned. The media ran stories about it for days. John Arlott wrote in the Observer *(He finds and reads a clipping)* that "No one of open mind will believe that he was left out for valid cricket reasons. In their selection, the MCC have stirred forces – for both good and evil – whose powers they do not truly comprehend."

And then, by another stroke of good fortune, a fortnight later, one of the selected players ruled himself out due to injury, and the MCC then had no choice but to select D'Oliveira after all. President Vorster restated that "this team of the Anti-Apartheid Movement will not be welcome in South Africa." The MCC couldn't back down now, and finally called off the tour.

And through it all, D'Oliveira himself remained silent, letting his bat do his talking in his innings for Worcestershire. Always elegant in his whites, while Vorster and his government were exposed to the world with their khaki trousers down around their lily white ankles. Basil was like a caged bird who had found freedom and soared skyward, floating gracefully on the cool breezes above England's pitches, above the test grounds in the West Indies, and Pakistan and Australia, but never in his native South Africa, where millions of his countrymen are caged still.

Song: I WISH I KNOW HOW IT FEELS TO BE FREE

> I wish I could be like a bird in the sky
> How sweet it would be if I found I could fly

> Well I'd soar to the sun and look down at the sea
> And I'd sing 'cos I know how it feels to be free
> Yes, I'd sing 'cos I know how it feels to be free
> Oh, I'd sing 'cos I know how it feels to be free

(Piano continues for a few bars, then stops at SOWANDE'S request)

I was awoken by a phone call from Lagos, at 2.10am that same night. My mother had died peacefully in her sleep earlier that evening, as I was making my way back from the Oval. I had received a letter from her only three weeks before, saying she thought she was not long for this world, and imploring me to come home quickly to see her one last time. I had booked a ticket immediately, but when to go? I had a case finishing in a fortnight, and I hoped, assumed I could travel two days after the Oval Test the week after that. In the end, I arrived two days too late.

(Pause)

I sang at the funeral. I needed to. My brother Fẹla accompanied me on the organ, in a Yoruba song titled simply Iya, (Mother), which asks God to bless an ever caring, loving mother.

Song: IYA

> Ko s'ẹni t'o feran mi, t'o mọ aini mi
> T'o ṣi le pese fun mi
> Bi iya mi, iya mi, iya mi
> Ko s'ẹni t'o feran mi,

> Ko s'ẹni t'o feran mi, t'o mọ aini mi
> K'Oluwa k'o gbe ọ o

Ladi Williams was in my flat again one day that October, to watch the Mexico Olympics. Marjorie, my, er, flat mate and house keeper and I had just fed him, again. Marjorie is sweet, but she found Ladi "a tiresome, pompous, verbose know-it-all." To be fair, he could go on all night if you let him.

This evening, he was explaining why the Biafran war had been inevitable – "Nigeria is a ridiculous, senseless, insensitive commercial construct of the British Empire. The two so-called protectorates – North and South – had been acquired by force and by bare-faced deceit – *deceit* – and merged together with no thought given to what the people in the North thought about those in the South. Or what those in the South West thought of those in the South East, not to talk of the North West and North East. They were just all lumped together, *bamm*, and told to pledge allegiance to the King without complaint! How is such an entity supposed to function properly after independence? How? When it should have been clear to anybody who had eyes to see that there was already distrust, ethnicity, infighting, regionalism and rivalry throughout. But after decades of anti-colonial struggle, the Brits were forced to say, 'You want independence? Ok, here you are. You are now independent Nigeria. Thank you, good bye. Oh, and by the way, just make sure that everything continues to flow through our banks and our companies to the coast, for us.

And that oil that they have found in the Niger Delta? Don't worry, BP and Shell will take care of that, thank you very much.' In 1966, there were two coups within six months – one by the Igbos, one by the Northerners. And then the Igbos want to secede, with all the oil. People are selling us arms from all over the world. Of course there'll be war!"

At this point, he shut up, because the 200 meters final was just getting underway. We were particularly interested in this race, because five of the eight runners were Black – three Americans, one Trinidadian and one Jamaican. We were hoping that Gold, Silver and Bronze would all be won by Black men. In the semi-finals, two of the Americans – John Carlos and Tommie Smith – were fastest. The Australian, Peter Norman was third fastest, but we hoped that the Trinidadian, Edwin Roberts would beat him and make it a Black one, two, three.

Interestingly, all the Black countries, and the Black Americans had wanted to boycott because South Africa were going, but eventually they were excluded, so the boycott was called off, although the Black Americans remained reluctant. In the end, thankfully, they too went, and here were some of them at the start of the final. Tommie Smith in Lane 3. John Carlos in 4. Peter Norman of Australia in 6 and Edwin Roberts of Trinidad in 8.

They're on their marks. All is silent. Set... Pow! And they're off. A great start by all. Difficult to say who's where as they run the bend, but Smith, Carlos, Norman and Roberts are all looking good. On to the straight. Carlos is ahead, followed by Smith. There's a gap before Norman and Roberts. With thirty meters to go, Smith pulls away. He's going to win it. Carlos is second, but Norman is catching up. Norman is closing in on Carlos! Come on, Carlos, come on, boy! Smith crosses the line. Roberts beats Carlos right on the line. Right on the line! So it's Smith first in 19.83 seconds, and a new World Record. Norman of Australia second, Carlos third, and Roberts of Trinidad fourth.

(Beat)

Well, two out of three isn't bad, really.

We didn't really watch the next few races, which was a bad mistake, because Ladi gets back into full flow about how there would be wars in other parts of Africa too in the coming years. Especially the Portuguese colonies.

(As Ladi:) Ok. Here is Portugal. This small area. In the scramble for Africa they ended up with five colonies. Five! Most of them bigger than themselves. You see white arrogance? Now, this big area here is Africa, and here, Angola. Their resistance movement is the MPLA under Augustinho Neto. Their armed wing is FAPLA. Socialist, Marxist-Leninist. There are also two Right wing movements – the FNLA and UNITA, under Jonas Savimbi. That is Angola, the most complex of the Portuguese colonies in Africa.

Here we have Mozambique. Their movement is FRELIMO, under Samora Machel.

Then, Guinea Bissau and Cape Verde, where you have the PAIGC, under Amilcar Cabral. Another great man.

Finally you have Sao Tome and Principe, and their liberation movement is the MLSTP, under Manuel de Pinto da Costa. I love that name!

Now, all the Leftist movements come together under the umbrella of the Conference of Nationalist Organisations of the Portuguese Colonies, CONCP.

So, on the Left you have CONCP comprising MPLA, FAPLA, FRELIMO, PAIGC and MLSTP, with support from the USSR, Cuba, GDR and others. And on the Right you have UNITA and FNLA, with support from the USA, South Africa, Saudi Arabia and Israel, all fighting the Portuguese. Now, if they win independence, there are three rival movements in Angola alone: UNITA, FNLA and MPLA. So you have what? Chaos, of course! And as Nigeria has shown us, that is a perfect recipe for? Civil war! Now, if you look at Central Afr... Are you not listening?"

The reason we were not listening was that the medal ceremony for the 200 meters was starting and the medal winners were making their way to the podium. Some respite from Ladi at last we thought, but no, he was off again.

"Foolish boys! You are a sell-out. You should have continued with the boycott, even unilaterally. You have to stick to your principles, whatever the cost. Now they are going to go home and make money with their gold and bronze. You have betrayed the memory of your ancestors and you have betrayed the future of children yet unborn. *Jọ!*"

(Piano plays The Star Spangled Banner) The Stars and Stripes started its slow rise up the pole. It was strange... the two Americans each had a fist in the air: Tommie Smith his right, John Carlos his left, each in a tight black glove. Their heads were bowed, as if in mourning. They seemed to have cut off the bottoms of their track suits to show black socks, and – look - no shoes!

A silent protest! As they made their way back towards the tunnel, you could hear some jeering and booing, but they walked on, heads held high, backs straight.

We looked at each other. Ladi opened his mouth, but then formed it into a smile, and nodded slowly. Enough said, already.

In interviews years later, Smith and Carlos would explain their protest in detail. Their black gloved fists were a gesture not just of Black Power, but human rights. John Carlos had his track suit top unzipped to signify solidarity with working class people worldwide, and to reveal a black T-shirt covering the letters USA on his vest – to signify the shame he felt in his country. His long necklace of beads honoured the thousands who had been thrown overboard into the Atlantic during the Middle Passage, or were lynched in America, even to this day. The black socks and shoeless feet represented the ongoing poverty of Black Americans. They both wore large OPHR badges – Olympic Project for Human Rights, the boycott organisation – and very poignantly, so too did Peter Norman, the White Australian.

Here were two sons of Africa and one son of Europe, standing there as equals, having shown human physical exertion at its most beautiful. Fair, healthy competition. But with the invention of the gun, the rifle, the European had triumphed over the African to such an extent that his descendants would end up on completely the opposite side of the globe from whence their ancestors had come. The White man tried, it seems, to wipe out the peoples he found in the Americas: North, Middle and South, and in Australia – another country founded on cruelty: cruelty in the way thousands were transported there against their will – as convicts from Britain; cruelty toward the Aboriginals who were slaughtered in their thousands, their lands stolen, the survivors enslaved and treated like animals. The Maoris in New Zealand fared marginally better.

Yes, Peter Norman was clearly more aware of, and troubled by his nation's history than most, for him to take that stand with the Black Americans. It was therefore absolutely appropriate (I humbly submit) that he should be up there on the podium, and not the Trinidadian, because it showed to the world that this white man recognised a legitimate demand for human rights, and that this white man fully understood that White people have a place in their struggle too. It made the protest somehow more poignant, more beautiful.

Song: HOLD ON. KEEP YOUR HAND ON THE PLOUGH

> The only thing that we did wrong
> Was stay in the wilderness a day too long
> Keep your eyes on the prize
> Hold On!

> But the one thing we did right
> Was the day that we started to fight
> Keep your eyes on the prize
> Hold on!
> Hold on, Hold on!
> Keep your eyes on the prize
> Hold on!
> Keep your eyes on the prize
> Hold on!

One evening in May 1969, I attended a rally at Friends Meeting House in Euston, London, called to discuss the proposed 1970 tour of the South African Cricket Test Team to England. I was amazed to see so many people there, of all colours! One young white man, barely twenty, South African from his accent, got up, and introduced himself as Peter Hain. He called it an affront for the MCC to announce such a tour barely months after the D'Oliveira Affair, and suggested that the same message that South Africa had sent to England had to be sent back to them – "You are NOT welcome." He floated the idea of direct action: taking active steps to prevent the tour from happening, and invited any interested parties to meet him afterwards. He got a huge round of applause. That was definitely the highlight of the evening.

I wished I could have been a student again. Hain's group, called the Stop The Seventy Tour was officially launched four months after, and set about disrupting the Springboks Rugby tour in October, throwing it into complete chaos.

And then on January 20, 1970, the nation woke up to widespread news coverage of coordinated attacks on practically every county cricket ground in the country. Slogans had been daubed on the grounds, "Don't Play With Apartheid!" Weed-killer poured on the outfield here, turf dug up there. It was as though they had been coached by *Umkonto We Sizwe* – the armed wing of the ANC! It seemed no cricket ground was safe, so guards and dogs were deployed, and Lord's was surrounded with thousands of meters of barbed wire! Eventually the MCC cancelled the tour.

Other sports would suffer too: Davis Cup tennis, athletics, swimming, wrestling and gymnastics, as well as business investments into South Africa.

(Beat)

From my modest flat in the Inner Temple, I tried to keep abreast of things happening in South Africa and other parts of the Continent. Much of it was depressing. Amilcar Cabral was assassinated in Guinea Bissau in 1973, and as Ladi had predicted, civil wars erupted in the Portuguese colonies. Nigeria's Head of State, Murtala Muhammed was assassinated six months into his premiership in January 1976 while carrying out sweeping anti-corruption measures. Seventy seven children were gunned down in the Soweto Massacre in June '76, and then in '77, Steve Biko became one of hundreds killed in police custody. Why? Why?

(Pause)

Song: SENZENI NA? (WHAT HAVE WE DONE) (A capella)

> *What have we done? / Senzeni na? Senzeni na?*
> *What have we done? / Senzeni na? Senzeni na?*
> *What have we done? / Senzeni na? Senzeni na?*
> *What have we done? / Senzeni na? Senzeni na?*

(Beat)

Muhammed's assassination convinced me that the decision I had taken after our mother's funeral had been the right one. We had taken her back to the village. I hadn't been there in over twenty years. It was much as I remembered it, though there were more cars around now. There were even some old ones abandoned right there in the village square. I had had a fantasy which now seemed ridiculous in 1968, even if it had seemed possible before I left in 1945: I would retire right here, to live again the simple life I had known as a boy. I would bring with me some cricket equipment, and teach the children the game. I would watch them play until the sun set, then I would drink palm wine and exchange stories with the other elders into the night. Learn about our ancestors. Speak the language. I would build a house big enough for Ayọ and Tunde to visit with their families from time to time. That would be so nice.

(Beat)

Tunde and I bonded again after the funeral. We had looked into each other's tear-filled eyes from either side of Mama's open casket. Our tears told us we each wished we had had more time with her while she was still with us. We talked later. Actually talked. No shouting this time. He was teaching. He had met someone he thought he would marry. I hoped I could meet her, and children too, one day. I hoped that he would make a better job of marriage, and yes, fatherhood than I had, and that we would have more time together in future.

(Beat)

Back in Lagos, the shouting started again.

(Beat)

As I looked out of the aeroplane window over Lagos the following week, recalling the village square littered with rusting Volkswagens and Citroens, the stray dogs, goats and chickens, I knew that my dream of return had just been buried along with my mother.

Song: TWO LITTLE WORDS

> Two little words so full of love and pain
> Oh, what a world of meaning they contain
> God be with you until we meet again,
> Till then, Good bye, Good bye.

Isn't it interesting, talking of my Nigerian village square, that the equivalent in any one of the Caribbean islands would actually have exactly the scene I imagined, with boys playing cricket with the most basic improvised equipment. Just what was it that made the game flourish there and not in Nigeria? It will take a much cleverer man than I to analyse and explain it, but one should be grateful for the forces – for good or evil – that meant that the West Indies would develop into the greatest of all cricketing nations in the 1970s, up to now. The decade started with the preeminence of Sir Garfield Sobers – one of the greatest all-rounders ever. As he bowed out, the young ones had come along – Clive Lloyd, Gordon Greenidge, Richie Richardson, Desmond Haynes, and Vivian Richards, from Antigua. What a player! I was present at one of his finest innings, one of the finest innings in recent cricketing history, at Lord's, and I watched it from the members' stand.

Oh yes – I became a member of the MCC in December 1976. In all my years as an ordinary spectator, I had seen very few Black people in the members' stand, including Sir Learrie Constantine and C L R James. I heard that the committee had decided to increase the membership from 16,000 to 18,000, to raise money for some refurbishments, so I applied. I assumed that my Yoruba name was going to be a problem, but I did have two pretty formidable members as proposer and seconder: Proposed by His Honour Judge J B Hobson QC; Seconded by His Honour Judge E Clarke, QC, and six months later, I found a brown envelope on my doormat, marked Marylebone Cricket Club, and enclosed therein was my FULL membership card.

(Sings)

    When I get to heabn', gonna put on my shoes...

I had been into the members area a few times before that, once with Ayọ, on one of her visits to London in 1954. Nigeria were playing the MCC, and some of us Nigerians were specially invited. I remember her surprise and disappointment that the Nigerian team was all white – colonial officers, professionals and businessmen. I also remember seeing these two white men eyeing my twelve-year-old daughter in a way that I imagined some plantation owners assessing young slave girls, for, for...

(Beat)

Ayọ and I were always close, but not so with Tunde. I haven't heard from him in eight years. Not since he sent me a clear message. I hadn't met his children, and I sent them air tickets to visit me, and this *(he picks up the envelope he had found earlier)* came back from Tunde. *(He brings out its contents: two air tickets neatly torn in half.)*

My boy had grown up. The world was smaller now. His life had been offered to me as a gift, and I had dropped the simplest of catches. And you know the biggest sleight? Tunde went to King's College too, but refused to play cricket...

(Beat. He replaces the envelope)

So, to the match at Lord's. June 23rd 1979. The final of the One Day International Series. The West Indies had beaten India, New Zealand and Pakistan. South Africa were still banned, and here were the West Indies meeting their former colonial masters at Lord's. It started quite badly for the Windies. They batted first, and lost four wickets for 99. Enter Collis King to join Viv Richards in the middle. King blasts away all over the pitch, scoring 86 from only 66 balls, before being caught by Randall. Ten fours and three sixes.

An explosive innings by this young tiger which even Viv Richards, then the greatest batsman in the world happily played second fiddle to.

(He picks up the bat and relives the game) Then, even with the last wickets all tumbling cheaply around him, Richards himself opens up, gets his characteristic swagger going, chewing on his gum, reaches his century and continues to pile on the runs in his ruthlessly, aggressively beautiful style. Boundaries in all directions. Now the final ball of the innings. He smashes it over deep square leg for six, and runs off the ground with Croft, to tremendous applause. The West Indies were 286 for 9, 138 of those coming off the bat of Vivian Richards.

England would have to score 287 to win – at 4.85 runs an over. Against one of the quickest bowling line-ups of all time: the Fearsome Four: Andy Roberts, Colin Croft, "Big Bird," Joel Garner, and "Whispering Death," Michael Holding, all capable of bowling at over ninety miles an hour.

The West Indian supporters, in all their colours, their noise, their music, became a formidable addition to the fielding team. It was all too much for England, and they were all out for 194.

The West Indies were champions of the world again. Blacks in the stadium, all over England, in fact all over the Commonwealth were ecstatic. Those eleven men had made as eloquent an anti-colonialist, anti-imperialist statement as any that had ever been made, and they had made it with great artistry – with the very tools their former masters had given them – the bat and the ball, and with that which God had given them – their brains.

Song: DAY – TIME FOR MAN GO HOME

> The monkey a bush bawl kwa, kwa, kwa
> Time for man go home
> Time for man go home
> Time for man go home

After the match, I was in the members' bar, enjoying a sherry with a friend, when I spotted Judge Harman, a fellow member at the Hurlingham Club. Long retired, but in fine health. A very loud and jovial man, you could hear him from across the room, in conversation with this old gentleman, all hunched up and clutching a carved walking stick. He had a young nurse or carer with him. Clearly of an African father, he had a look of a young Tunde about him...

As I approached them, Judge Harman bellowed, "Well I never. I knew you'd be here! How the devil are you? I say, Edgar, Old Boy, do you know this reprobate?"

I realised I was once more in the presence of Edgar Mappin Esq. His MCC blazer was old and worn, and messy with food and spit. Grey stubble on his chin, few teeth left. I caught a definite flash of panic in his eyes before he composed himself, looked back at Judge Harman and said, "Er, No."

I recalled that morning in 1954, at Castlemount Chambers. Me in my worn suit, fantasising about discussing cricket with him over sherry. I could barely string three words together before stumbling out of his chambers into London's cold streets. Now, knowing I was among the most finely turned out people there that evening, in my new MCC blazer and bow tie, in my new status as Part-time Crown Court Judge, I said, "Your Honour, I remember meeting you very briefly, many years ago. Ọlatunji Ṣowande is the name. Ọlatunji Ṣowande"

He knew that he had played the ball, and had got the faintest of nicks. I had caught it, but he hadn't walked, like any decent cricketer would have, as every schoolboy, be he in London or Lagos, in Canberra or Calcutta, Auckland or Ahmedabad, is taught: "You get a nick, you walk. You get a nick, you walk."

I was now at the crease, he the bowler. A fine ball, headed for my middle stump. The half second it took to reach me was time aplenty. My bat was already lifted. I had brought it down straight, shoulders open, wrists relaxed, and with an easy, elegant swing, I had middled it perfectly, sending it back over his head, over long-on, over the boundary, beyond the boundary, to the other side of the globe. The best, the sweetest, the most satisfying stroke I had ever played. Ever.

As he is describing this, he plays the stroke in slow motion, points skyward over the audience, following the path of the imaginary ball, then clenches his upheld hand into a fist, and bows his head, with the bat in his other hand. As lights fade slowly to black, we realise that he has in fact taken his shoes off.

The clock ticks on.

CLOSE OF PLAY

The following music is used in the play:

The Holy City
Composed by Stephen Adams.
Lyrics by Frederic Wetherley.
Publisher: Boosey & Hawkes

Deep River
Trad. Arranged by Harry T Burleigh
Publisher: Ricordi

I Dream A World
Composed by William Grant Still.
Lyrics by Langston Hughes
Publisher: William Grant Still Music

I Wish I Knew How It Would Feel To Be Free
Composed by Billy Taylor
Lyrics by Billy Taylor and Dick Dallas
Publisher: Duane Music Inc.

Iya
Composed, and Lyrics by Ayọ Bankọle
Publisher: University of Ifẹ Press

The Star Spangled Banner (Instrumental)
Composed by John Stafford Smith
Publisher: Longman & Broderip

Hold On
Trad. Arranged by Margaret Bonds
Publisher: Theodore Presser Co.

Two Little Words
Composed by May H. Brahe
Lyrics by Helen Taylor
Publisher: Boosey & Hawkes

Time For Man Go Home
Trad. Arranged by Max Saunders
Publisher: Boosey & Hawkes